I0143394

Beyond Bethlehem and Calvary

*12 Dramas
for Christmas, Easter,
and More!*

Diana C. Derringer

CSS Publishing Company, Inc.
Lima, Ohio

BEYOND BETHLEHEM AND CALVARY

FIRST EDITION
Copyright © 2015
by CSS Publishing Co., Inc.

For more information about CSS Publishing Company resources, visit our website at www.csspub.com, email us at csr@csspub.com, or call (800) 241-4056.

e-book:
ISBN-13: 978-0-7880-2810-6
ISBN-10: 0-7880-2810-3

ISBN-13: 978-0-7880-2809-0
ISBN-10: 0-7880-2809-X

PRINTED IN USA

Beyond Bethlehem and Calvary is dedicated
to family and friends who pray for my written words,
to drama teams who put those words into action,
and, above all, to my Savior, the eternal word of life.

Table of Contents

Mary's Song

* * *

Time: 4-5 minutes

Theme: Christmas, Jesus as Messiah, praise

Scripture Reference: Luke 1:39-56

Church Year Season: Christmas

Suggested Use: Christmas program, sermon starter

Summary: Mary, after learning she will be the mother of Jesus, visits Elizabeth, who is six month's pregnant.

Characters
Mary — a teenage girl
Elizabeth — Mary's cousin, an older girl

Props: A clay water jar

Costumes: Floor length tunics and head coverings

Sound: Two wireless mics

Lighting: General stage

Setting: Zechariah and Elizabeth's home in the hill country of Judea

* * *

Elizabeth enters stage area from one side, carrying the water jar on her shoulder. From the opposite side, Mary runs to her, breathless, with arms extended. As Mary nears, Elizabeth lowers the jar to the floor and embraces her.

Mary: (*steps back*) Oh, Elizabeth, I'm so happy to see you, and I have the most amazing news!

Elizabeth: (*Startled, she lays her arm across her abdomen and then speaks in a loud voice.*) Blessed are you among women, and blessed is the fruit of your womb. And why has this happened to me, that the mother of my Lord comes to me? For as soon as I heard the sound of your greeting, the child in my womb leaped for joy. And blessed is she who believed that there would be a fulfillment of what was spoken to her by the Lord (Luke 1:42-45).

Mary: (*raises hands to sides of face*) You know, don't you? Isn't it amazing? (*lowers hands*) I was so scared when the angel appeared. And when he told me that, because of God's favor, I would bear the Son of God and was to name him Jesus... can you imagine my confusion? Joseph and I weren't married yet. Sure, we were pledged to one another, but definitely not married! (*pauses*) Yet, Gabriel assured me that the power of the Holy Spirit would make this possible. Then he told me that you, my dear cousin, would have a baby soon! Can you believe it? After all these years...

But, oh my, I had so many questions. (*begins counting on fingers*) What would people say? Would Joseph understand? What would happen if he didn't? What kind of mother would I be to the Son of God? Yet, I believe we're to follow as God leads.

As soon as Gabriel left (*grasps Elizabeth's arms*), I had to see you to share the miracle in both our lives. (*slower, with concern*) Please pray for me, Elizabeth. I want to be worthy. I must be prepared for my task.

Elizabeth: (*hugs Mary*) Of course I'll pray for you. And I know God will provide whatever you need for this special plan.

Mary: Thank you. What would I do without you? (*steps away from Elizabeth and toward audience, lifts eyes and arms, either sings "The Magnificat" or quotes the following*)

My soul magnifies the Lord, and my spirit rejoices in God my Savior, for he has looked with favor on the lowliness of his servant. Surely, from now on all generations will call me blessed; for the mighty one has done great things for me, and holy is his name. His mercy is for those who fear him from generation to generation. He has shown strength with his arm; he has scattered the proud in the thoughts of their hearts. He has brought down the powerful from their thrones, and lifted up the lowly; he has filled the hungry with good things, and sent the rich away empty. He has helped his servant Israel, in remembrance of his mercy, according to the promise he made to our ancestors, to Abraham and to his descendants forever (Luke 1:46-55).

Mary returns to Elizabeth's side. They wrap their arms around one another's waist and exit, talking quietly with heads close together.

(*lights out*)

A Bouquet of Praise

*** * *

Time: 2 minutes

Theme: Easter, thanksgiving, praise

Scripture Reference: Ephesians 1:3-10; Psalm 100:1-5

Church Year Season: Easter, thanksgiving, any

Suggested Use: Children's Easter program, sermon starter

Summary: Children lay flowers at the foot of a cross and thank Jesus for the blessings in their lives.

Characters
Child 1 — boy or girl
Child 2 — boy or girl
Child 3 — boy or girl
Child 4 — boy or girl
Child 5 — boy or girl

Props: A cross, five Easter lilies

Costumes: Contemporary dress clothes

Sound: Five wireless mics

Lighting: Spotlight on area around cross

Setting: Church stage

* * *

The cross stands center stage. One by one the children enter, face the side of the cross so their profile is to the audience, share words of thanks, lay a lily at the foot of the cross, and exit the other side.

Child 1: Thank you, Jesus, for being with me when I was sick. I want to help others like you helped me.

Child 2: Thank you, Jesus, for a family that loves me. Help me to always love others as I should.

Child 3: I'm sorry, Jesus, that I don't always act the way I should. Thank you for forgiving me.

Child 4: Thank you, Jesus, for giving your life for me. I want to live my life for you.

Child 5: I'm so glad, Jesus, you rose from the dead and that I'll someday have a home in heaven with you. Help me tell others, so they can know you too.

(lights out)

Eggsactly

* * *

Time: 2 minutes

Theme: Easter, forgiveness, unconditional love

Scripture Reference: John 3:16-17

Church Year Season: Easter

Suggested Use: Children's Easter program, sermon starter, community outreach

Summary: Children share God's love for us exactly as we are.

Characters
Child 1 — boy or girl
Child 2 — boy or girl
Child 3 — boy or girl
Child 4 — boy or girl

Props: Four large posters with "EGGSACTLY" in bold, colorful letters surrounded by painted Easter eggs

Costumes: Contemporary dress clothes

Sound: Four wireless mics

Lighting: General stage

Setting: Any

Director's Notes: Ease of performance makes this ideal for either a church or community setting.

* * *

Children stand center stage, facing the audience. Their posters are turned toward them with the blank side facing the audience.

Child 1: I don't always listen when I should, but God loves me eggsactly as I am.

All: (*turn signs and repeat together*) Eggsactly! (*turn signs back toward selves*)

Child 2: I sometimes run when I should sit, but God loves me eggsactly as I am.

All: (*turn signs and repeat together*) Eggsactly! (*turn signs back toward selves*)

Child 3: I'm not always as sweet as I look now, but God loves me eggsactly as I am.

All: (*turn signs and repeat together*) Eggsactly! (*turn signs back toward selves*)

Child 4: When I lose my temper, I say things I shouldn't say, but God loves me eggsactly as I am.

All: (*turn signs and repeat together*) Eggsactly! (*turn signs back toward selves*)

Child 1: No one is perfect. We all mess up sometimes.

Child 2: But God loves us. That's why Jesus died on the cross for our sins.

Child 3: When Jesus rose again on the third day, he defeated sin and death.

Child 4: If we give Jesus control of our lives, he forgives us and promises he will be with us forever.

All: That's eggsactly what Easter's all about. (*turn signs and repeat together a little louder*) Eggsactly! (*freeze briefly before exiting*)

Optional Ending: *Sing "He's Still Workin' On Me."*

(*lights out*)

Making a Message

*** * ***

Time: 7 minutes

Theme: Christmas

Scripture Reference: Luke 2:17

Church Year Season: Christmas

Suggested Use: Children's Christmas program, sermon starter

Summary: Children make paper Christmas ornaments with a message.

Characters
Mom — older girl
Child 1 — boy or girl
Child 2 — boy or girl
Child 3 — boy or girl

Props: Table with four chairs; paper, crayons or markers; child safety scissors; hole punch; paper ornaments of a star, wise man, angel, shepherd, sheep, camel, donkey, Mary, Joseph, Jesus in a manger, a candy cane; small Christmas tree; and ornament hangers

Costumes: Casual contemporary clothing

Sound: Four wireless mics

Lighting: General stage

Setting: Family room

* * *

Children sit around the table coloring as Mom brings the tree on stage.

Mom: Okay gang, what's the progress report on your ornaments?

Child 1: I'm almost finished with my last one!

Mom: Wow! That's fast! How about the rest of you?

Child 2: Not much longer, if I can get all these stripes the same.

Mom: Aha! You must be working on a candy cane, huh?

Child 2: Yes, and it's harder to make than I thought.

Mom: (*looks over Child 2's shoulder*) I'm sure you'll get it. (*walks behind Child 3 and places hands on shoulders*) What's that you're working on?

Child 3: (*covers paper with hand*) It's a secret. I'll show you when I'm finished.

Mom: (*raises hands from shoulders*) Okay. No problem. I'll just get our hangers ready while you finish. (*Mom begins humming "Away In A Manger." Children join on one verse while they complete their work.*)

Child 3: I'm ready now!

Mom: All right, why don't you start with one of yours. (*hands him a hanger*)

Child 3: I've made a star like the one that guided the wise men to baby Jesus.

Mom: Very good. I guess that needs to go on top, doesn't it?

(*Everyone nods. Child 3 places star.*)

Mom: (*looks toward Child 2*) Your turn. Choose one of yours.

Child 2: Well, I guess I'll put a wise man on to go with the star. (*gets hanger from Mom and hangs ornament*)

Mom: Good choice. (*looks toward Child 1*) What's first for you?

Child 1: I have an angel. Remember the angels told the shepherds that Jesus was born.

Mom: I certainly do remember. Does anyone have a shepherd?

Child 2: I have one!

Child 3: And I have a sheep.

Mom: Great! Why don't we put them on at the same time, since they all fit together in the Christmas story. (*Mom hands a hanger to each child. After all are hung, Mom props her* *hand under her chin.*) Hmmm… We have the star and a wise man, an angel with a sheep and shepherd. What do we need next?

Child 3: Hey, the wise man needs a camel to ride. I made a camel. (*runs to table, gets hanger from Mom, hangs ornament*)

Mom: Okay! Look at the work we've already done. What now?

Child 3: How about a donkey? Didn't Mary ride a donkey?

Mom: Good point. Although the Bible doesn't actually say Mary rode a donkey, most people think she probably did. Since you've had all our other animals, I suppose you have one of those too?

Child 3: I do. You want it now?

Mom: Sure, why not? Of course, that means we need …

Children: (*unison*) Mary!

Child 1: I have her and Joseph! (*runs to get ornaments*)

Child 2: And I have baby Jesus in a manger. (*gets ornament*)

Mom: We definitely need to put them on the tree, don't we? After all, without Jesus' birth we wouldn't celebrate Christmas. (*Mom gives hangers. After ornaments are hung, all stand back to admire their work.*) Are we finished?

Child 2: What about my candy cane?

Child 3: Silly, a candy cane isn't part of the Christmas story.

Child 2: It is too. My Sunday school teacher told me so.

Child 3: But, Mom, they didn't even have candy canes when Jesus was born.

Mom: That's true, but why don't we see how the teacher explained it? (*looks to Child 2*) Can you tell us?

Child 2: Sure. She said the candy cane helps us remember why Jesus came. The red reminds us how Jesus shed his blood on the cross to pay for our sins. The white shows that when we ask Jesus to forgive us and come into our lives, he washes us white as snow. Then when we hold the candy cane with the crook at the top (*demonstrates*), it looks like a shepherd's staff. That means Jesus guides us and protects us like a shepherd does his sheep. When we hold the candy cane upside down (*demonstrates*), it looks like the letter "J," the first letter in Jesus' name. And the sweet flavor makes us think of God's love. (*big smile*)

Mom: Great explanation, I think your candy cane's a perfect addition to our tree. After all, Christmas tells only part of the story of God's love. (*Child 2 gets a hanger and puts cane on tree.*)

Child 1: Hey, Mom. Can we leave our tree up until Easter? That way it will remind us every day why Jesus came.

Child 1 and 2: Please, Mom, please?

Mom: (*laughs*) We'll have to think about that, but we definitely need to remember daily why Jesus came and thank him for his love. Why don't we do that right now? (*Family holds hands, forms a circle around the tree, and bows heads.*) We thank you, God, for your love and for sending Jesus as our Savior. Help us share your love wherever we go. Amen.

Children: Amen!

(*lights out*)

Let His Light Shine

* * *

Time: About 15 minutes

Theme: Christmas, humility

Scripture Reference: Luke 2:1-20; Matthew 2:1-2, 9-11; Romans 12:3

Church Year Season: Christmas

Suggested Use: Children's Christmas program, sermon starter

Summary: Two stars, after bragging about their greatness on the night of Jesus' birth, receive a reminder of the greatest one and everyone's purpose in relationship to him.

Characters
Star 1 — boy or girl
Star 2 — boy or girl
Star 3 — boy or girl, older and taller than Star 1 and Star 2
Narrator — offstage
Joseph 1 — older boy
Mary 1 — older girl
Baby Jesus — baby or life-size doll
Shepherd 1 — boy
Shepherd 2 — boy
Joseph 2 — older boy
Mary 2 — older girl
Toddler Jesus — two-year-old boy
Wise Man 1 — boy

Wise Man 2 — boy
Wise Man 3 — boy

Props: An elevated area behind center stage; staffs for the shepherds; a bale of hay; a manger filled with straw and strips of cloth; a rough hewn, bench-size block of wood; small roughly carved wood animals; gifts to represent gold, incense, and myrrh

Costumes: Three star costumes with glow-in-the-dark front strips; plain long tunics with head coverings for Mary, Joseph, and the shepherds; long cloths to wrap baby Jesus; long tunics and crowns in royal colors (purple, gold, red) for the wise men

Sound: Three wireless mics for Stars, offstage mic for Narrator

Lighting: A spotlight for each scene

Setting: The sky over Bethlehem; Jesus' birthplace; and, about two years later, outside the home of Joseph and Mary

✳ ✳ ✳

Scene 1

The Stars, on the elevated stage, wave their arms in various directions as they move about. If no glow-in-the-dark strips are available, focus the spotlight on them.

Star 1: Blink. Blink. Look at me! Look at me! No star can outshine me.

Star 2: You think you're so great. Just look at this: Blink! Blink! Blink!

Star 3: Watch out now. You don't want to fall. We have lots of stars in the sky, each with a special job to do.

Star 1: Yeah, I know, but none can match the way I shine! Get a load of this sparkle: Blink! Blink! Blink!

Star 2: Hah! That's nothing. Anyone following you on a dark night would be in big trouble. My twinkling, on the other hand, would get them right where they need to go.

Star 1: Brag, brag, brag. You don't have a clue, do you?

Star 3: I keep telling you two that you need to back off. You're going to take a tumble if you're not careful.

Star 2: Back off yourself, old timer. You've been around so long you're getting dull around the edges. We'll have to put you in the back part of the sky before long.

Star 1: Ha! (*high fives Star 2*) You finally said something right! Don't let it go to your head, though. My brilliance still puts yours to shame.

Star 2: That's what you think. Remember the song all the children play and sing? (*begins singing and dancing to "Twinkle Twinkle Little Star"*) That song was written about none other than (*great emphasis and bow*) *moi.*

Star 3: (*shakes head*) Dear me. Dear me. The Creator must be so disappointed.

Star 2: (*gazes down*) Whoa! (*pauses*) What's going on down there?

Star 1: (*looks down and around*) What? Where? I don't see anything?

Star 2: (*points*) Look to your right. See? There in Bethlehem?

Star 1: (*with wonder and reverence*) Oh my! The promised one has been born. (*confused, wanders around the stage, wrings hands*) What do we do? What do we do? Somebody please remind me what we do!

Star 2: (*scratches head and roams*) A lesson ... I remember a lesson ... a couple hundred years ago. (*whines*) But it's been so long! Why can't I remember the directions?

Star 3: (*calmly and with authority*) Stand aside young ones. We can't keep the world waiting any longer. After all these years, they need someone to guide them to their Savior. (*steps forward as the other Stars turn their backs so only Star 3's glow can be seen, raises head and prays*) Heavenly Father, may my light reflect your glory as it shines on your promised one. (*pauses, then turns away from audience so glow fades*)

Scene 2

Spotlight to left of center stage. Joseph 1 stands beside Mary 1, who sits on the bale of hay. Mary 1 picks up Baby Jesus from the manger and cuddles him. The Narrator begins reading Luke 2:1-20. When verse 8 begins, the Shepherds walk toward the family, kneeling before them. Slowly the spotlight focuses only on Baby Jesus. As the reading concludes, the spotlight fades.

Scene 3

Spotlight to the right of center stage. Joseph 2 and Mary 2 sit together on the large block of wood, smiling at Toddler Jesus, who's sitting on the ground, playing with the small wooden animals. Occasionally Joseph 2 joins him briefly. As the Narrator begins reading Matthew 2:1-12, Star 3 turns and moves behind the family. The Wise Men enter, carrying their gifts. One at a time they kneel before Toddler Jesus, presenting their gifts. The spotlight gradually focuses only on Toddler Jesus, but Star 3 remains in place. The scene freezes.

Narrator: (*after a lengthy pause*) God creates each of us with a special role to perform — the stars, Mary and Joseph, the shepherds, the wise men (*pauses*), and you. But whatever we do, rather than focusing on ourselves and our accomplishments, our primary task will always be to reflect the light and love of Jesus so others can find their way to him.

(*lights out*)

Don't Look Back:
A Grandparent's Story

* * *

Time: 3 minutes

Theme: Past vs. present living

Scripture Reference: Genesis 19:12-29

Church Year Season: Any

Suggested Use: Sermon starter, group discussion

Summary: A grandparent, using the story of Lot's wife, encourages a grandchild not to dwell on the past.

Character
Grandparent — boy or girl

Props: A rocker and small table near center stage, telephone

Costume: Comfortable, everyday clothing for an older person

Sound: One wireless mic

Lighting: General stage

Setting: Family room

* * *

Grandparent sits in rocker, talking on telephone.

Trust me, sweetheart, we need to leave the past in the past. We can get caught up so easily in regretting what might have been or longing for previous good times. I'm not saying we should rid ourselves of memories, but we don't need to get so bogged down in the past that we forget to live in the here and now.

The Bible gives a good illustration in the story of Lot and his family. They lived in the area of Sodom and Gomorrah, and honey (*waves hand forward*), the people around there were definitely not the sort you want for neighbors. They took sin to new heights!

Finally, the Lord decided enough was enough. Before destroying the cities, however, he sent word to Lot and his family to get out of Sodom and (*extra emphasis*) get out fast. They didn't want to be there when judgment came! Lot and his wife had two daughters, both pledged to be married. However, when Lot tried to advise their young men to leave with them (*brushes hand along opposite arm and turns head up and to the side*) they ignored old Lot, brushed his concern off as a joke, and never moved an inch!

Once outside the city, an angel warned the family to run for their lives and not look back. As they escaped, the sun came up (*raises hand*), and fire and sulfur rained down (*lowers hand*). Whether from curiosity, regret, or some other reason, Lot's wife looked back. The Bible tells us that, because of her disobedience, she turned into a pillar of salt.

Now I can't explain all about that or claim I understand it. Yet this much I do know: God told her not to look back and she didn't listen.

Does this mean we shouldn't learn from the past? Of course not! Unfortunately, far too many people remain focused on yesterday and forget what needs to be done today.

You listen to your old grandma (or grandpa). The past is past, and you can't do anything about it. (*strong emphasis*) But you do have today, and you can do something about that.

Well, I have to go now. You take care and stay in touch. I love you.

(*lights out*)

Love Bears All Things

* * *

Time: 5 minutes

Theme: Christmas, grief, love

Scripture Reference: Colossians 3:12-14; Matthew 18:1-4

Church Year Season: Christmas

Suggested Use: Christmas Service, sermon, or group discussion starter

Purpose: To demonstrate the impact of pure and simple love

Summary: A child shares her most prized possession with a hurting adult.

Characters
Mother — older girl
Sarah — preschool girl
Aileen — older girl
Judith — older girl

Props: Two benches sitting at an angle near one another, several full shopping bags, a small stuffed bear, facial tissue

Costumes: Contemporary winter clothing

Sound: Four wireless mics

Lighting: General stage

Setting: Benches inside a mall

Director's Notes: We tend to complicate love when simplicity often shows it best. Allow a child to demonstrate. Although written for the Christmas season, this script can be used any time of year with a few minor alterations.

* * *

Mother and Sarah enter, holding hands. Sarah hugs her bear to her chest and skips to an empty bench where they sit. Mother lowers her packages to the floor. Aileen and Judith enter from the opposite side at the same time and sit on the other bench. They also lower their packages and sigh simultaneously. They smile at the young family and listen in amusement to their conversation.

Mother: Wow, this feels good. My feet were getting tired, weren't yours?

Sarah: Nope, my feet feel good (*holds bear out and looks at him*), but poor Mr. Snuggles needed a rest… and he's getting hungry too! (*holds bear close again*)

Mother: Okay, love. We'll let Mr. Snuggles rest a few minutes and then see what we can find for lunch.

Sarah: Mr. Snuggles really hopes he gets some ice cream for dessert.

(*Aileen and Judith look at one another and laugh quietly, Judith with her hand over her mouth.*)

Mother: We'll see, love, we'll see.

(*Mother puts her arm around Sarah, who lays her head against Mother, and closes her eyes. Mr. Snuggles remains tight against Sarah's chest.*)

Aileen: (*deep sigh*) How I wish I could be so carefree again.

Judith: You've had a rough time lately, haven't you Aileen?

Aileen: That's just part of life I guess, but sometimes I wonder how much more I can take. When my husband died last year I thought life couldn't get worse. (*shakes head*) Little did I know. (*silence for several seconds and then with sobs catching in throat*) A child and grandchild are supposed to outlive their mother!

(*Sarah wiggles around and opens her eyes so she has a clear view of Aileen.*)

Judith: I know. (*pats Aileen's arm*) I know.

Aileen: God promised never to give us more than we can bear, but I'll never get to share another Christmas with them. No more birthdays. No babysitting. Oh, Judith, Christmas is the hardest of all! (*lowers head and sobs while Judith pats her back*)

(*Sarah sits up; her lower lip begins to quiver.*)

Aileen: (*wipes eyes with a tissue from her pocket*) I'll be okay. I just miss them so much. Megan used to climb up in my lap, hug my neck, and say, "I love you, Nana." (*tears *start again but with a smile*) There's nothing sweeter in the world than a little one's love.

Sarah: (*slowly moves toward Aileen*) What happened to Megan?

Mother: Sarah, it's not polite to ask such questions.

Aileen: (*smiles while speaking to Mother*) No, dear, that's okay. (*turns attention to Sarah, pats the seat beside her*) A few months ago Megan and her mother were on their way to my house when we had a terrible flood. Megan's mother tried to cross a bridge that wasn't safe. Signs were up to say no one should cross, but Megan's mother tried anyway.

Sarah: (*gets on her knees and pats Aileen's face*) So now you're sad?

Aileen: Yes, now I'm sad. But I still have wonderful memories of our time together, and that helps me not be so sad. (*smiles weakly*)

Sarah: How old was Megan?

Aileen: She was about your age and a sweet girl like you.

Sarah: Did she have a bear named Mr. Snuggles?

Aileen: She had a bear, but his name was just Bear.

Sarah: Oh. (*brief pause*) Will holding Mr. Snuggles make you feel better?

Aileen: You know, I think that might make me feel much better.

Sarah: (*hands him over*) Here you go, Mr. Snuggles.

Aileen: Thank you, Sarah. I feel better already.

Sarah: (*slowly crawls onto Aileen's lap and wraps both arms around her neck*) I love you, Megan's Nana. Merry Christmas. (*lays head on shoulder*)

Aileen: (*hugs Sarah tightly, fights tears*) Merry Christmas, Sarah. Merry Christmas!

(*lights out*)

A Rabbit's Tale

* * *

Time: 4 minutes

Theme: Easter, salvation

Scripture Reference: John 19:17-18; John 12:32; Hebrews 12:2

Church Year Season: Easter, any

Suggested Use: Children's worship service, Easter service, sermon starter

Purpose: To examine the meaning of the cross

Summary: A rabbit's encounter with a cross leaves it wondering why anyone would find beauty in it.

Character
Rabbit

Props: Three crosses on one side of the stage, a carrot

Costume: Bunny ears or a full rabbit costume

Sound: One wireless mic

Lighting: General stage

Setting: Outdoor crucifixion scene

Director's Notes: We find a wide range of crosses, from the beautiful to the rustic, used today for home décor or fine jewelry. They also appear on bumper stickers, billboards, and other public venues. Many churches display them on steeples or the side of their buildings. But what message do they give to those unfamiliar with the story of Jesus? This script invites us to rethink a central symbol of our faith.

∗ ∗ ∗

From the exit opposite the crosses, the rabbit hops out, holding a carrot in one hand and humming "Here Comes Peter Cottontail." He stops occasionally to nibble on the carrot or twitch his nose while looking around. As he hops near the crosses, he suddenly bumps into the middle one.

Ouch! What a strange place to plant a tree. (*slowly looks up at the cross*) Come to think of it, what a strange looking tree. (*hops around the cross*) No leaves… hmmm… strange, very strange. (*looks up and down again*) No limbs to speak of either, unless you count that one big one up there that goes straight across. (*scratches head*) Interesting, very interesting…

(*sits down and leans against the middle cross, wiggles around and changes positions several times, nibbles on the carrot with each new position*) Good grief! This thing certainly leaves a body feeling mighty uncomfortable. You'd think it would at least provide a cushy spot to prop and do nothing for a while. (*tries crossing legs, leans lower, slides to the floor with head against the cross*) Nope, this just won't work. No resting on my laurels around this hunk of wood. I guess I might as well get up and try to do something useful… (*stands up and twitches nose*) or not.

(*looks back and forth at the other two crosses*) What do you know? Two more just like it. Whoever planted these must have a wicked taste in trees. All I can say is *Yuk*! Yet they do look a bit familiar. (scratches head, looks down with hand under chin, moves around) Hmmm... I can't place when and where...

(*suddenly jerks head up, faces audience, and shakes index finger*) I've got it! I've got it! Now I know where I've seen these — the top of those big buildings where people go on Sundays. I wonder if they stole their decorating idea from this stumpy looking stuff. Doesn't make sense to me though. (*places hand against the side of the center cross, crosses one leg over the other*) Why would they want to decorate anything to look like this ugly old tree? What kind of beauty can they find in it?

(*continues to look at the center cross, slowly moves away from and to the front of it, tilts head, pauses, and holds arms out to each side, forming a cross with the rabbit's body*) What kind of beauty, indeed!

Rabbit freezes, lights fade, and rabbit exits in the dark.

(*lights out*)

The Fishermen's Call

* * *

Time: 4 minutes

Theme: Resurrection, salvation, commitment

Scripture Reference: Matthew 4:18-22; 28:1-10

Church Year Season: Easter, any

Suggested Use: Easter service, sermon starter

Summary: Two fishermen discuss Peter, Andrew, James, and John's decision to follow Jesus, plus their own reaction to the man and his message.

Characters
Fisherman 1, acquaintance of Peter, Andrew, James, and John — older boy
Fisherman 2, acquaintance of Peter, Andrew, James, and John — older boy

Props: A stall made from wood and/or cloth, large fish nets, artificial fish

Costumes: Knee length or long tunics

Sound: Two wireless mics

Lighting: General stage

Setting: A Jerusalem street vendor's stall

Director's Notes: With Bibles and the story of Jesus readily available today, it's hard to imagine the questions and confusion many experienced during Jesus' time on earth. Put yourself inside the skin of ordinary citizens who try to understand this incredible time in history.

* * *

The Fishermen mend their nets as they talk and offer fresh fish for sale.

Fisherman 1: (*speaks to audience*) Shalom. Good day to you. Can I interest you in a mess of fresh fish? Just caught them myself this morning. (*allows time for a reply*) No? Well, if you're hungry later, we'll be here... unless we've sold them all, of course.

Fisherman 2: (*speaks to Fisherman 1*) You'd think with all the festivities going on, business would be better.

Fisherman 1: Ah, no need to despair. The day's still young. (*pauses but continues working on net*) Say, have you heard the latest about Peter and Andrew?

Fisherman 2: What about them?

Fisherman 1: They quit their fishing to follow that teacher, Jesus, the one crucified a few days ago.

Fisherman 2: I heard. At first I thought they'd surely lost their minds. I mean, why leave a good job, even if it does require hard work, to wander around after someone who has no apparent means of support? But it wasn't just Peter and

Andrew. Zebedee's two boys, James and John, quit everything to follow him too. They claim they're now fishers of men... whatever that means.

Fisherman 1: (*shakes head*) Strange...

Fisherman 2: That's what I thought at first but did you get a chance to hear the man teach?

Fisherman 1: Can't say that I did, not that I was interested anyway. Why do you ask?

Fisherman 2: Well, I don't know if I can explain it, but there was something different about him. He didn't try to get anyone's money. He showed compassion to everyone, even the bums, crazies, and down and outers. And his teaching wasn't so much about rules and traditions but about our relationship with God and one another. Of course that didn't sit so well with many of the religious leaders. You know them and their long lists of dos and don'ts and how to get around them when it suits their purposes.

Fisherman 1: Uh-huh.

Fisherman 2: Even when they arrested Jesus and beat him, he didn't fight back. I never could figure out why they crucified him in the first place. Seems to me that teaching and living the kind of life he did set a fine example for the rest of us. What do I know, though? I'm just a fisherman. Anyway, it seems a shame to me that a good man's life can be taken so easily.

Fisherman 1: There's a rumor going around that he rose from the dead.

Fisherman 2: Really? Hmmm… I stayed out fishing a little longer than usual this time, so I haven't talked to anyone since the day he died. I wouldn't be surprised though. Like I said earlier, there's something special about that one.

Fisherman 1: (*long pause, then turns toward audience*) Ah, fine day, isn't it, friend. Can I interest you in a mess of fresh fish? Caught them myself this morning.

(*lights out*)

Joseph and Mary's Boy

* * *

Time: 4 minutes

Theme: Jesus as Messiah, resurrection, proclamation

Scripture Reference: Luke 2:41-52; Matthew 28:6-7

Church Year Season: Easter

Suggested Use: Easter service, sermon starter

Summary: A neighbor of Joseph and Mary recalls Jesus' childhood, ministry, and events leading to his resurrection.

Character
Neighbor — boy or girl

Props: None

Costume: Long tunic and head covering

Sound: One wireless mic

Lighting: General stage

Setting: The streets of Jerusalem

Director's Notes: The Bible provides little information about Jesus' childhood. Imagine what life must have been like for someone who knew him from childhood and that person's response to his arrest, crucifixion, and resurrection.

* * *

Neighbor smiles, approaches the crowd, speaks in a conversational tone

Is this your first trip to Jerusalem? I've lost count of the number of times we've come. We try to make it for Passover every year. The travel time helps us catch up with the lives of our family and friends.

I remember well the year Joseph and Mary's boy was twelve. Always such a responsible young fellow, his behavior that year seemed especially strange. We had a fairly routine trip here but, let me tell you, our return home was anything but ordinary! After a full day's journey, Joseph and Mary couldn't find Jesus. They checked with everyone in our group, but no one had seen him all day.

Forgetting their fatigue, they immediately started backtracking. Three long days later, they finally found him. He had been with the teachers in the temple courts the entire time, listening, asking questions, and amazing everyone with his understanding. Of course, Joseph and Mary's ability to appreciate his maturity was a bit hampered at that point.

Until then I can't recall a single time Jesus' family questioned his behavior. When his parents told him to do something, he did it. If they told him not to do something, he didn't. He always requested permission for special activities. He tried not to offend the other boys, but at the same time, he had no qualms about standing up for what was right. (*laughs*) I still wonder why a little of his actions couldn't have rubbed off on my boys!

Anyway, back to the story: Jesus, puzzled at his parents' search, asked if they didn't realize he would be in his father's house. I doubt that anyone fully grasped the significance of that question at the time.

However, all that and more make perfect sense now. His life, his obedience, and his ministry of the last three years... everything began falling into place. Jesus, my young neighbor, my children's playmate... I still can't believe it... He's our Messiah!

Even harder to comprehend, however, is his recent mockery of a trial. I can't find any logical reason for such a miscarriage of justice. (*shakes head*) And then his cruel, senseless death... I might have believed it for someone else, but not Jesus — never Jesus.

(*face and voice brightens*) His tormentors' victory, however, was short lived. Three days after his crucifixion, Jesus burst that tomb wide open, and out he came! Ask around. Everyone's talking about it — some in whispers, others openly. Me? I'm ready to shout it from the rooftops!

(*ducks head and laughs*) I get a little carried away, don't I? I hope I haven't delayed you too long, but I just can't keep this good news to myself! Enjoy the rest of your journey. Shalom. Go in God's peace.

(*lights out*)

From Flawed to Free

***

Time: 3 to 4 minutes

Theme: Easter, redemption

Scripture Reference: Luke 23:32-43

Church Year Season: Easter, any

Suggested Use: Good Friday or Easter service, group discussion, sermon starter

Summary: The repentant thief speaks from his cross. His attitude mirrors the life transformation that occurred when he turned to Jesus.

Characters
Narrator — offstage
Thief on the Cross — offstage

Props: Three crosses

Sound: Two offstage mics for speakers

Lighting: Spotlight on center cross, with the other two crosses visible but in shadows

Setting: Calvary

***

Narrator: Have you ever wondered what went through the minds of the two men crucified with Jesus? While we hear from the repentant thief, our focus remains on the center cross, the source of his hope and ours.

As light focuses on the center cross, the voice of the repentant thief begins offstage. He speaks with a rough, uncaring attitude.

Well, I've proved them right, and I hope they're satisfied! Why should I care anyway? Nobody ever cared for me; that's for sure. Get them before they get me, that's what I always said. And I got 'em good. I got 'em real good! Nothin' mattered. Least of all those religious hypocrites with their fancy robes and their high and mighty ways. Oh, they sounded fine, but they didn't care if I lived or died. And now they stand there gawking, just waiting for me to die. I wanted to spit in their faces and yell, "You did this to me! People like me don't stand a chance."

I bet that guy on the third cross knows what I'm talkin' about. He's been yellin' and cussin' all day. (*pauses then speaks in puzzled voice*) Funny thing, though, most of it's been at the man on the middle cross. There's some kind of sign over the middle guy's head, and everybody keeps laughin' at him and callin' him king of the Jews. They yelled at him to save himself if he was the Son of God. (*skeptical*) What's this Son of God stuff? Humph! Didn't seem like much of a king to me, hangin' on a cross. So I gave him a mouthful too.

(*pauses then speaks slower and not as harshly*) But I've never seen anybody act like him. He didn't cuss or yell. He didn't fight back. And he kept sayin' stuff that didn't make a bit of sense — stuff about forgiveness and people not knowing what they were doin'. (*harsher*) Seemed to me they knew exactly what they were doin'. They were killin' us and laughin' while they did it!

(*calmer*) But the more I watched and listened, the more I wanted what he had. He was dyin' just like us, but... I don't know how to explain it. He seemed peaceful. (*in amazement*) Man, if he could be peaceful hangin' on a cross, what's goin' on? So I kept listenin' and the more everyone made fun of him and said he wasn't God's Son, the more convinced I became that was exactly who he was.

So I told the other guy to shut up. The two of us knew we'd end up here some day, but this man didn't deserve it. Then I asked the man, Jesus, to remember me, and he told me he would! For the first time in my life somebody promised somethin' I could believe. He said I'd be with him in paradise today. (*in awe*) Paradise, can you believe it? For a bum like me? Doesn't make sense, but I don't care. I trust Jesus with this worthless life — what little I have left.

(*lights out*)

The Greatest Daddy of All

* * *

Time: 4 minutes

Theme: Father's Day, parenting example

Scripture Reference: Ephesians 6:4

Church Year Season: Father's Day, any

Suggested Use: Father's Day program, sermon starter

Summary: Following his father's example, a child tells his friend about God's love and forgiveness.

Character
Young Boy — elementary school age

Props: None

Costume: Casual clothing for elementary-age boy, dirty tennis shoes, baseball cap

Sound: One wireless mic

Lighting: General stage

Setting: Any location

* * *

The Young Boy enters, hands in his pockets, and kicks an imaginary object. He stops near center stage.

There's a new kid at my school, and he told me he'd never been to church before and didn't know much about God. I thought (*with great expression*), wow, how sad! So I decided he needed to learn.

I told him how God created the whole world and the animals and plants and people. My friend thought that was pretty cool. (*pauses and smiles*) Then I explained about God's power — how God's stronger than the most powerful dynamite ever made. My friend said that was waaay cool. When he heard how God's Spirit can be with us all the time and be with people on the other side of the world too, my friend said he bet I made that up. But I said no, God really can do it.

He decided it would be something great if he had even half of God's knowledge after I said God knows everything. Thinking about that a little longer, he wondered if maybe he needed to change some of the words he says and the way he treats his little brother... especially since God's sort of like the biggest judge of all and wants us to act right. That scared my friend. But I told him God loves us, even the meanest person that ever lived. Plus God will forgive us if we're truly sorry. We just need to ask God to take charge of our lives.

Later my friend asked how I knew all this neat stuff, and I said, "That's easy, my daddy told me and showed me in the Bible." Then I told him my favorite part, how God's like the greatest daddy of all. God's Son, Jesus, had a special word for God. He called God *abba*, a word that's a lot like "daddy." Only God never forgets or makes mistakes or leaves us alone like some daddies. Calling God *abba* doesn't mean we don't respect God. It only means that we're close and God will always be there (*emphatically*) no matter what. (*pauses*)

After hearing all this, my friend decided he wanted God as his father too. (*big smile and pause*) (*heads toward exit, then turns back to audience*) I think my daddy must be taking lessons from God on how to do this father thing. I'm glad, because that's the kind of daddy I want to be when I grow up!

(*pauses then begins kicking at imaginary object again as exits*)

(*lights out*)